"BUGS" BOWER'S

Today's Wav

To Play™ The Stan s

for all keyboa

Edited by Professor Kathryn Stan.

Copyright © 1998, 2001 by Nancy Music Company, Inc.

All rights reserved. No part of this book may be reproduced in any form or by any electronic or mechanical means, including information storage and retrieval systems, without permission in writing from the publisher.

Order No. NM 10008
International Standard Book Number: 0.8256.4226.4

Exclusive Distributors:
Music Sales Corporation
257 Park Avenue South, New York, NY 10010 USA
Music Sales Limited
8/9 Frith Street, London W1D 3JB England
Music Sales Pty. Limited
120 Rothschild Street, Rosebery, Sydney, NSW 2018, Australia

Printed in the United States of America by
Vicks Lithograph and Printing Corporation

Nancy Music Company, Inc.
New York

AFTER YOU'VE GONE

Basic Rhythm

LEFT HAND CHORD CHART

Play one octave lower

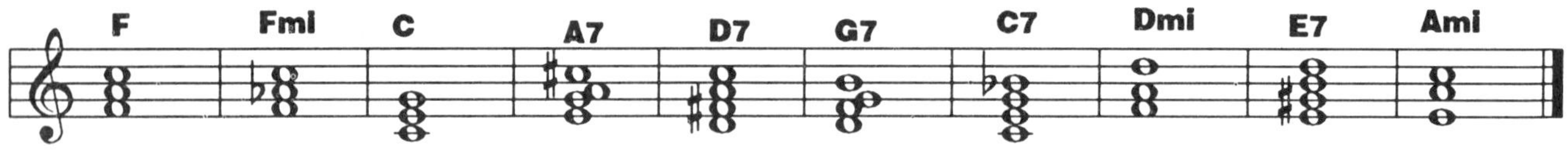

"AFTER YOU'VE GONE" Song & Chord Studies

These studies will develop a sense of harmony.

**** Note: REPEAT each STUDY until you know the NOTES in the CHORDS!***

AFTER YOU'VE GONE

LEFT HAND CHORD CHART

Play one octave lower

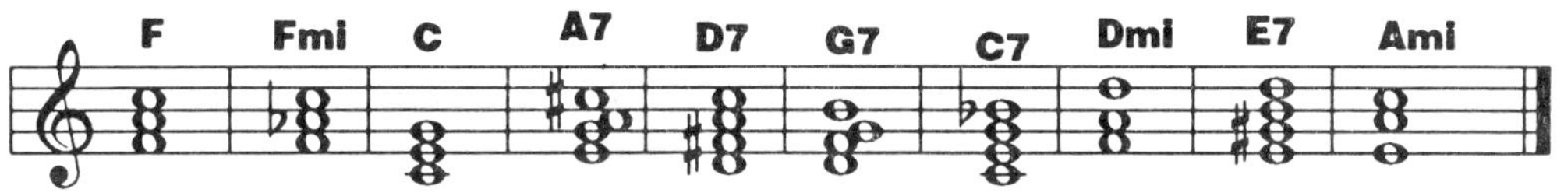

NANCY MUSIC CO. INC. COPYRIGHT 1998

ALEXANDER'S RAGTIME BAND

Basic Rhythm

LEFT HAND CHORD CHART

Play one octave lower

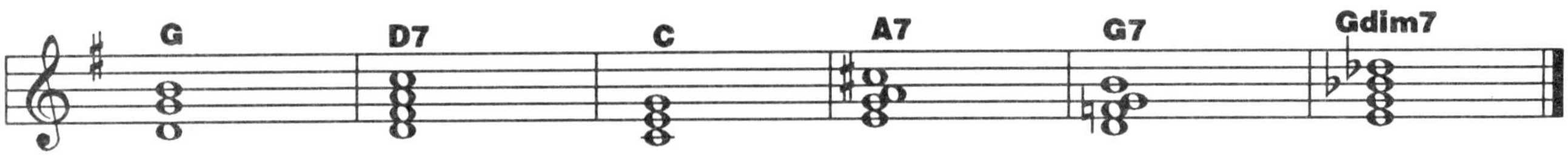

"ALEXANDER'S RAGTIME BAND" Song & Chord Studies

These studies will develop a sense of harmony.

SONG---- ***CHORDS----***

**** Note: REPEAT each STUDY until you know the NOTES in the CHORDS!***

ALEXANDER'S RAGTIME BAND

LEFT HAND CHORD CHART

Play one octave lower

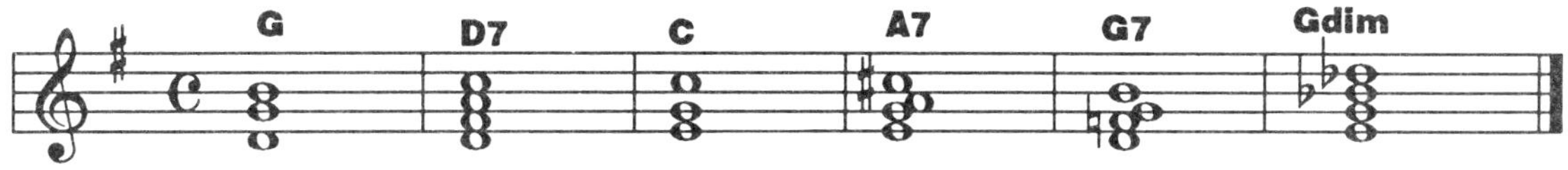

NANCY MUSIC CO. INC. COPYRIGHT 1998

ALICE BLUE GOWN

Basic Rhythm

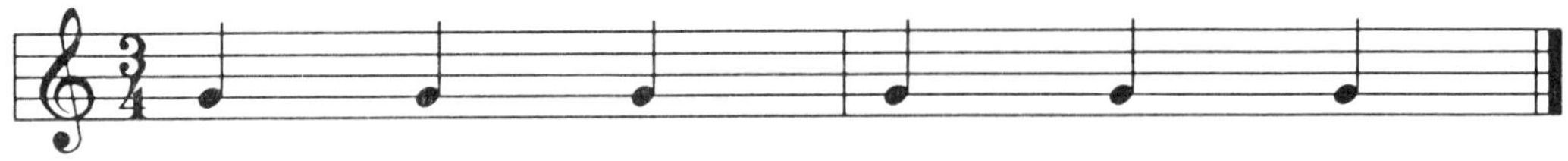

LEFT HAND CHORD CHART

Play one octave lower

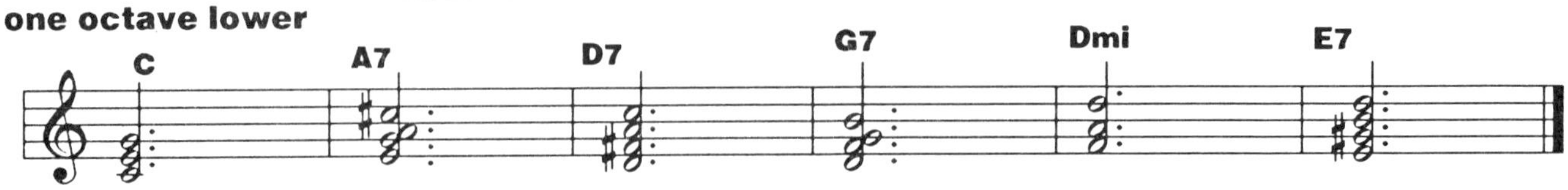

"ALICE BLUE GOWN" Song & Chord Studies *

These studies will develop a sense of harmony.

*** Note: REPEAT each STUDY until you know the NOTES in the CHORDS!**

ALICE BLUE GOWN

LEFT HAND CHORD CHART

Play one octave lower

NANCY MUSIC CO. INC. COPYRIGHT 1998

APPLE BLOSSOM TIME

Basic Rhythm

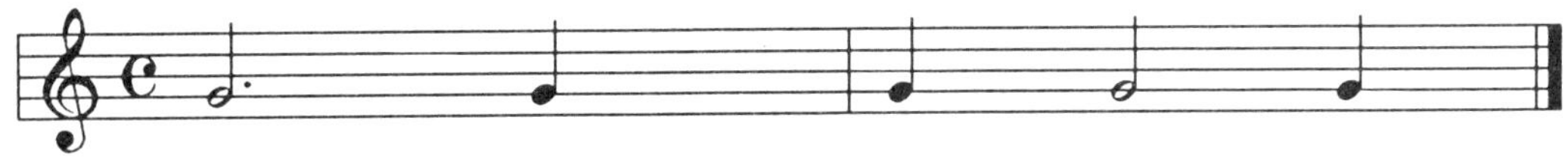

LEFT HAND CHORD CHART

Play one octave lower

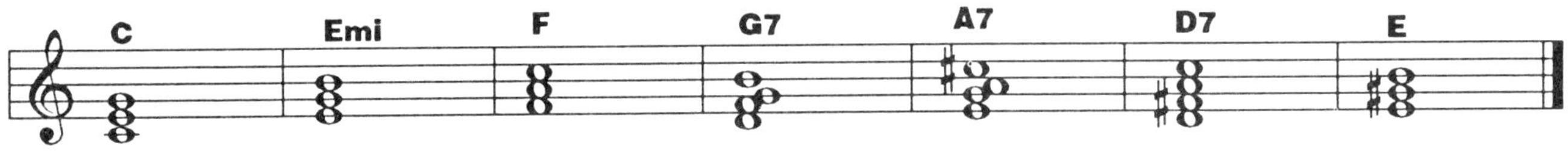

*"APPLE BLOSSOM TIME" Song & Chord Studies **

<u>These studies will develop a sense of harmony.</u>

** Note: REPEAT each STUDY until you know the NOTES in the CHORDS!*

APPLE BLOSSOM TIME

LEFT HAND CHORD CHART

Play one octave lower

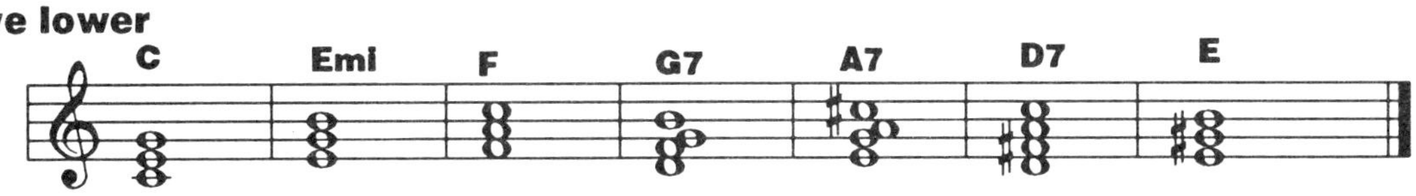

NANCY MUSIC CO. INC. COPYRIGHT 1998

APRIL SHOWERS

Basic Rhythm

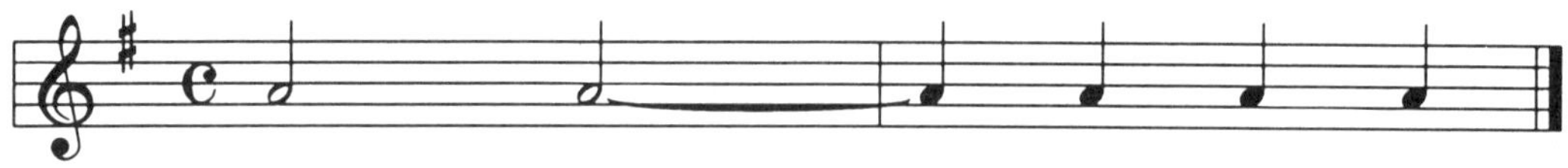

LEFT HAND CHORD CHART

Play one octave lower

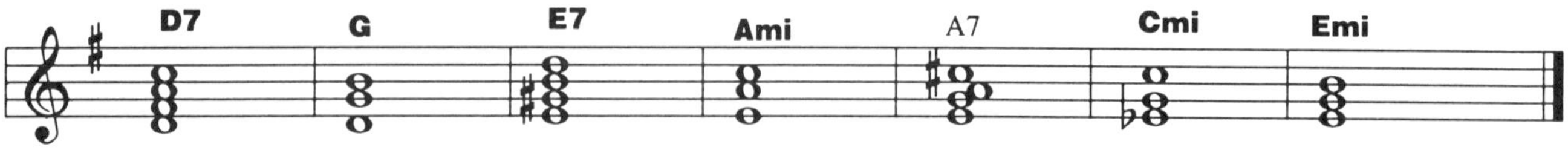

*"APRIL SHOWERS" Song & Chord Studies**

These studies will develop a sense of harmony.

***** Note: REPEAT each STUDY until you know the NOTES in the CHORDS!***

APRIL SHOWERS

LEFT HAND CHORD CHART

Play one octave lower

NANCY MUSIC CO. INC. COPYRIGHT 1998

AURA LEE

Basic Rhythm

LEFT HAND CHORD CHART

Play one octave lower

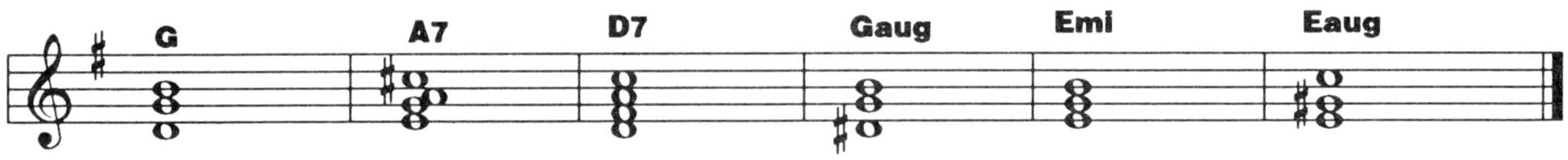

*"AURA LEE" Song & Chord Studies **

These studies will develop a sense of harmony.

** Note: REPEAT each STUDY until you know the NOTES in the CHORDS!*

AURA LEE

LEFT HAND CHORD CHART

Play one octave lower

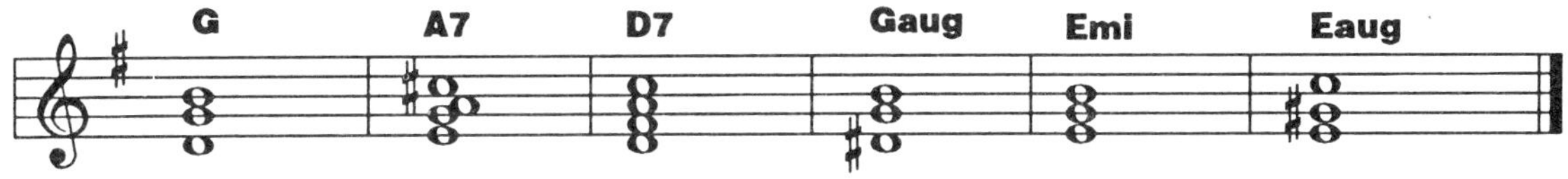

NANCY MUSIC CO. INC. COPYRIGHT C 1998

AVALON

Basic Rhythm

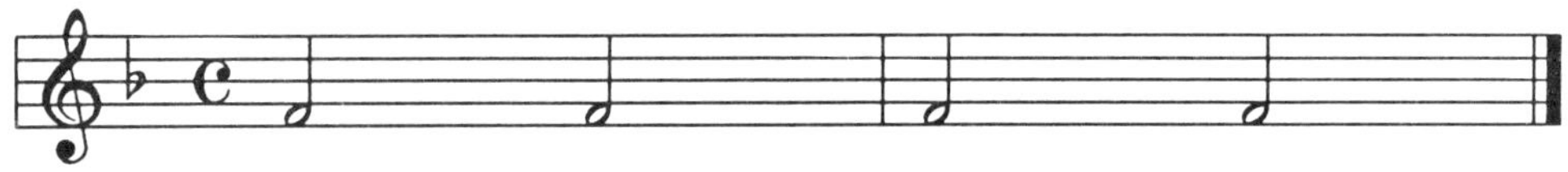

LEFT HAND CHORD CHART

Play one octave lower

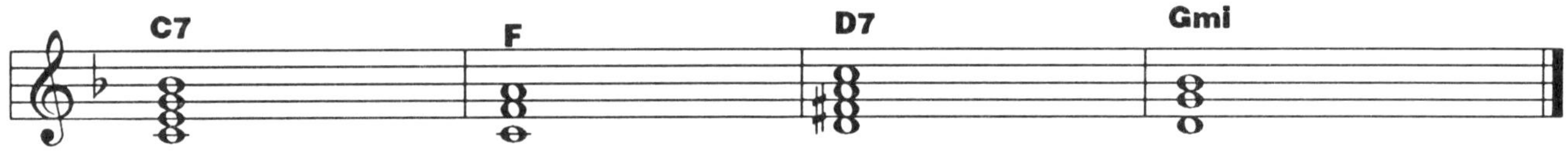

*"AVALON" Song & Chord Studies**

These studies will develop a sense of harmony.

SONG---- **CHORDS----**

*** Note: REPEAT each STUDY until you know the NOTES in the CHORDS!***

AVALON

LEFT HAND CHORD CHART

Play one octave lower

NANCY MUSIC CO. INC. COPYRIGHT 1998

BALLIN' THE JACK

Basic Rhythm

LEFT HAND CHORD CHART

Play one octave lower

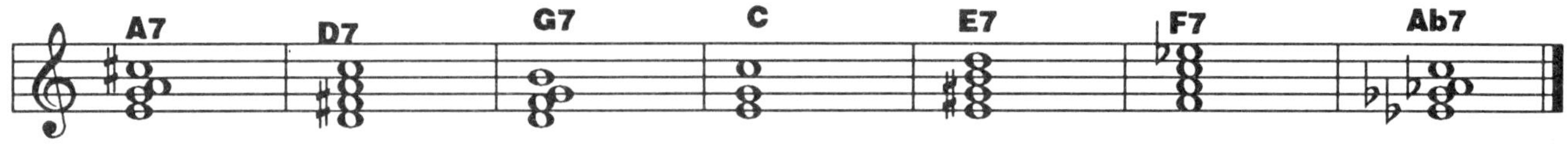

"BALLIN' THE JACK" Song & Chord Studies *

These studies will develop a sense of harmony.

SONG---- ***CHORDS----***

**** Note: REPEAT each STUDY until you know the NOTES in the CHORDS!***

BALLIN' THE JACK

LEFT HAND CHORD CHART

Play one octave lower

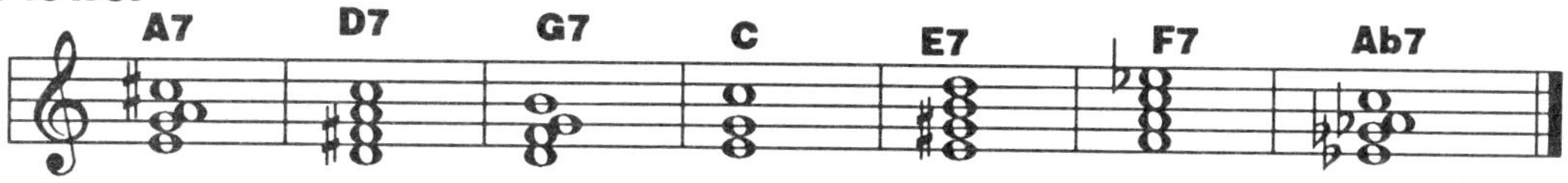

NANCY MUSIC CO. INC. COPYRIGHT 1998

BEAUTIFUL OHIO

Basic Rhythm

LEFT HAND CHORD CHART

Play one octave lower

*"BEAUTIFUL OHIO" Song & Chord Studies **

<u>These studies will develop a sense of harmony.</u>

** Note: REPEAT each STUDY until you know the NOTES in the CHORDS!*

BEAUTIFUL OHIO

LEFT HAND CHORD CHART

Play one octave lower

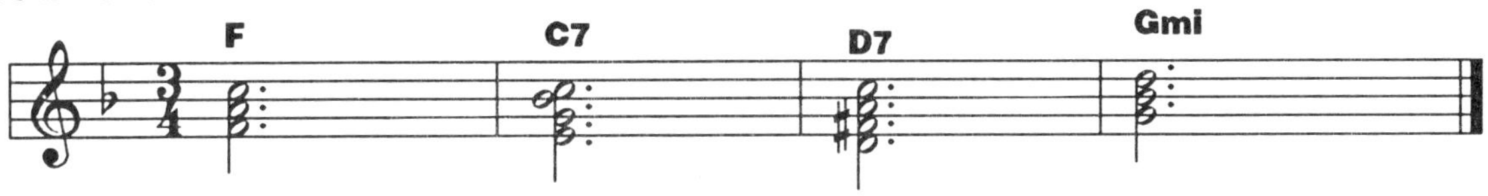

NANCY MUSIC CO. INC. COPYRIGHT C 1998

BY THE LIGHT OF THE SILVERY MOON

Basic Rhythm

LEFT HAND CHORD CHART

Play one octave lower

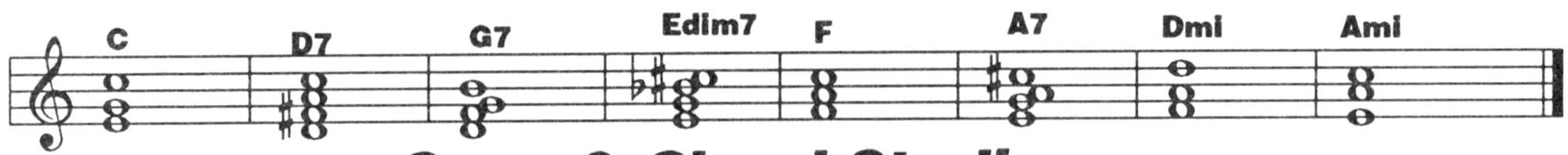

Song & Chord Studies

These studies will develop a sense of harmony.

**** Note: REPEAT each STUDY until you know the NOTES in the CHORDS!***

BY THE LIGHT OF THE SILVERY MOON

LEFT HAND CHORD CHART

Play one octave lower

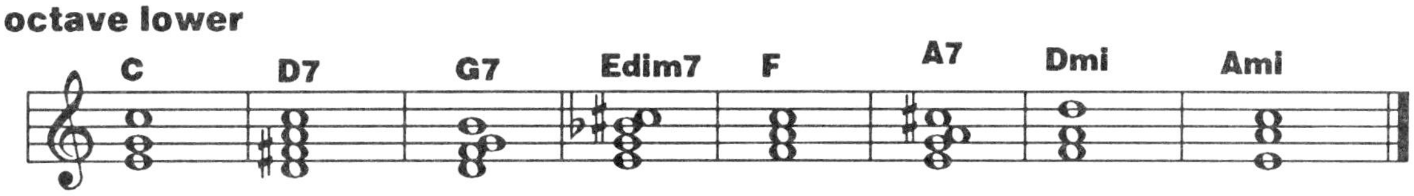

NANCY MUSIC CO. INC. COPYRIGHT C 1998

CHICAGO

Basic Rhythm

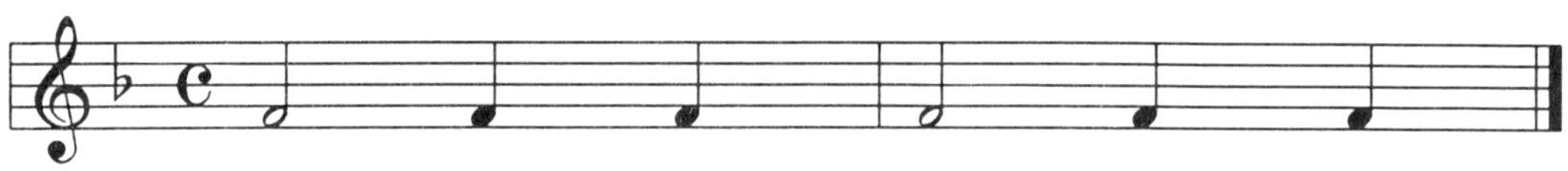

LEFT HAND CHORD CHART

Play one octave lower

*"CHICAGO" Song & Chord Studies**

These studies will develop a sense of harmony.

**** Note: REPEAT each STUDY until you know the NOTES in the CHORDS!***

CHICAGO

LEFT HAND CHORD CHART

Play one octave lower

NANCY MUSIC CO. INC. COPYRIGHT 1998

CUDDLE UP A LITTLE CLOSER

Basic Rhythm

LEFT HAND CHORD CHART

Play one octave lower

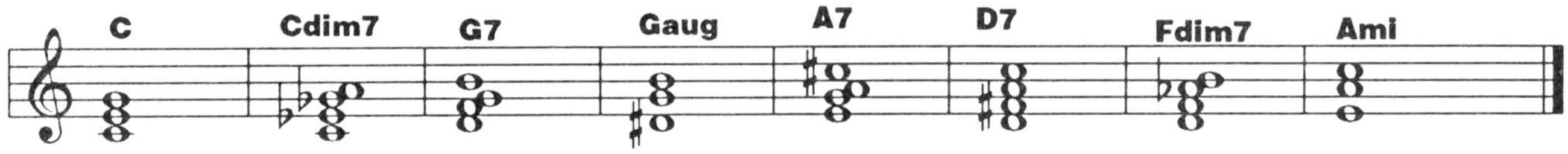

Song & Chord Studies

These studies will develop a sense of harmony.

*** Note: REPEAT each STUDY until you know the NOTES in the CHORDS!***

CUDDLE UP A LITTLE CLOSER

LEFT HAND CHORD CHART

Play one octave lower

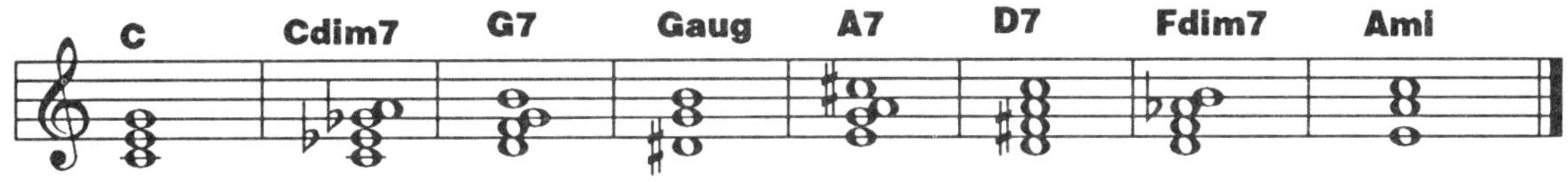

NANCY MUSIC CO. INC. COPYRIGHT C 1998

DARK TOWN STRUTTER'S BALL

Basic Rhythm

LEFT HAND CHORD CHART

Play one octave lower

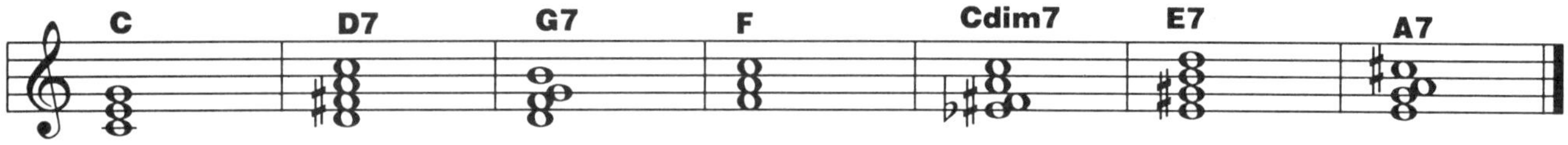

"DARK TOWN STRUTTER'S " Song & Chord Studies

These studies will develop a sense of harmony.

SONG---- ***CHORDS----***

**** Note: REPEAT each STUDY until you know the NOTES in the CHORDS!***

DARK TOWN STRUTTER'S BALL

LEFT HAND CHORD CHART

Play one octave lower

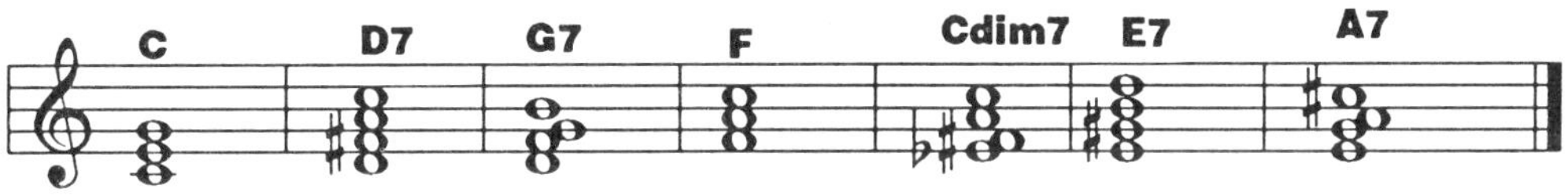

NANCY MUSIC CO. INC. COPYRIGHT 1998

DO YOU EVER THINK OF ME

Basic Rhythm

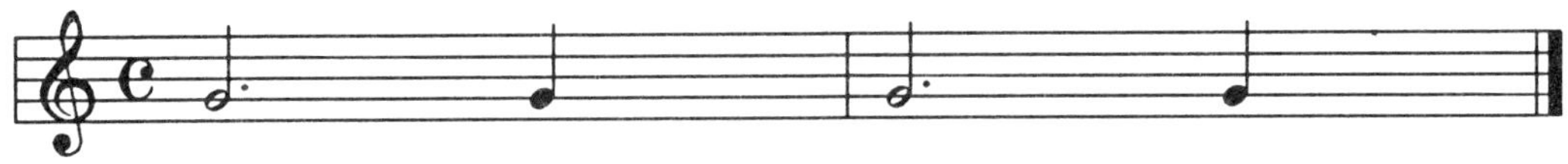

LEFT HAND CHORD CHART

Play one octave lower

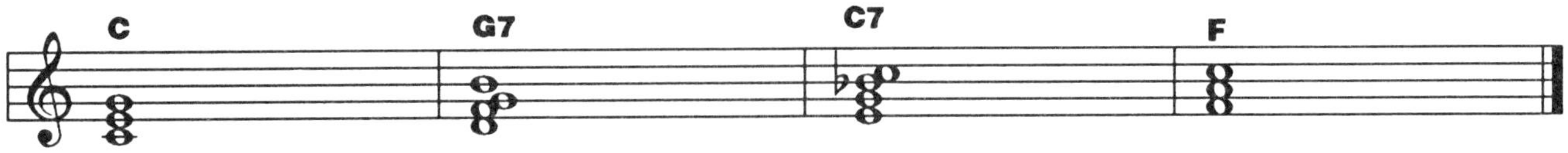

"DO YOU EVER THINK OF ME" Song & Chord Studies

These studies will develop a sense of harmony.

*** Note: REPEAT each STUDY until you know the NOTES in the CHORDS!***

DO YOU EVER THINK OF ME

LEFT HAND CHORD CHART

Play one octave lower

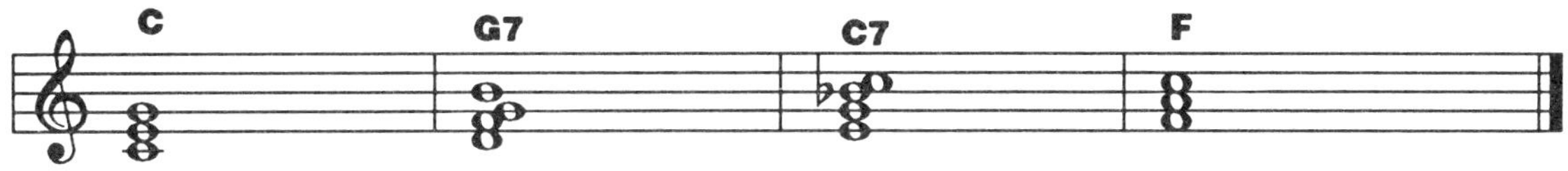

NANCY MUSIC CO. INC. COPYRIGHT C 1998

EVERY LITTLE MOVEMENT

Basic Rhythm

LEFT HAND CHORD CHART

Play one octave lower

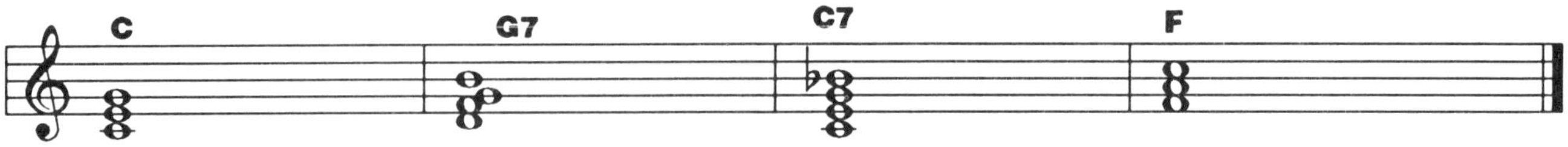

Song & Chord Studies

These studies will develop a sense of harmony.

SONG---- **CHORDS----**

**** Note: REPEAT each STUDY until you know the NOTES in the CHORDS!***

EVERY LITTLE MOVEMENT

LEFT HAND CHORD CHART

Play one octave lower

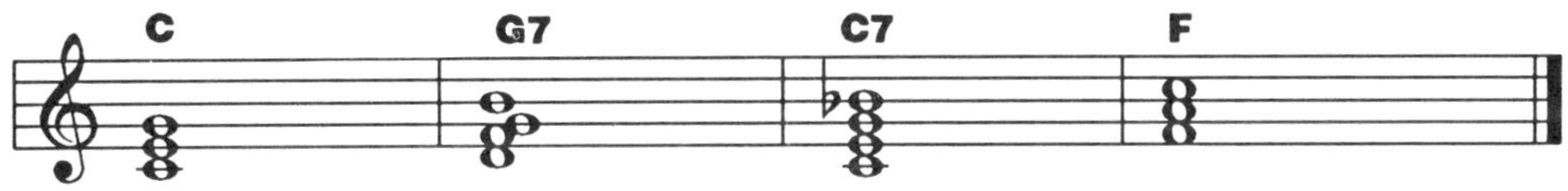

NANCY MUSIC CO. INC. COPYRIGHT 1998

FOR ME AND MY GAL

Basic Rhythm

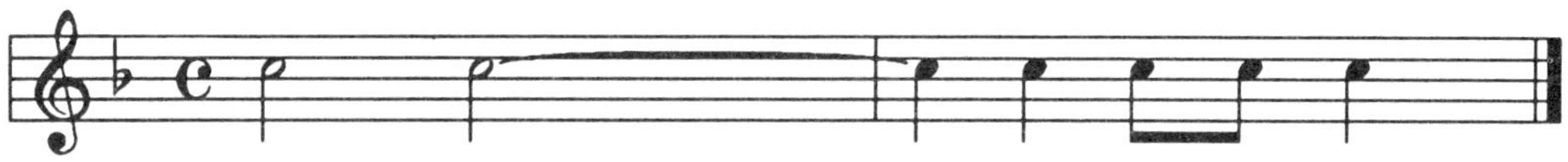

LEFT HAND CHORD CHART

Play one octave lower

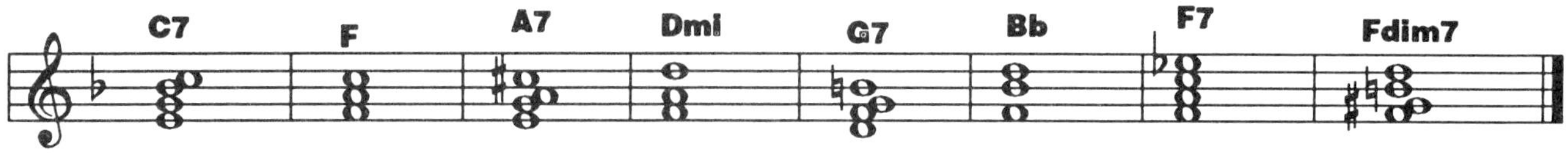

*"FOR ME AND MY GAL" Song & Chord Studies**

These studies will develop a sense of harmony.

** Note: REPEAT each STUDY until you know the NOTES in the CHORDS!*

FOR ME AND MY GAL

LEFT HAND CHORD CHART

Play one octave lower

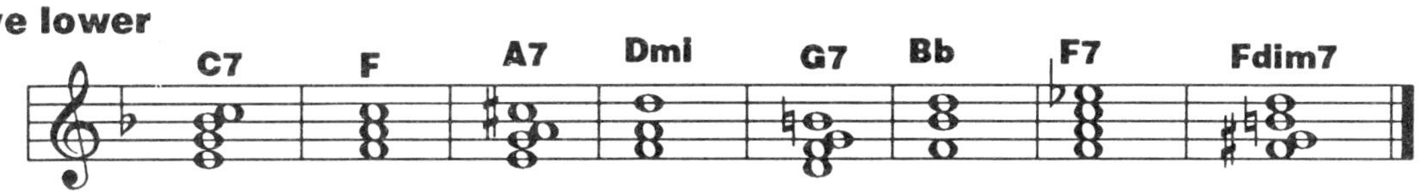

NANCY MUSIC CO. INC. COPYRIGHT 1998

I AIN'T GOT NOBODY

Basic Rhythm

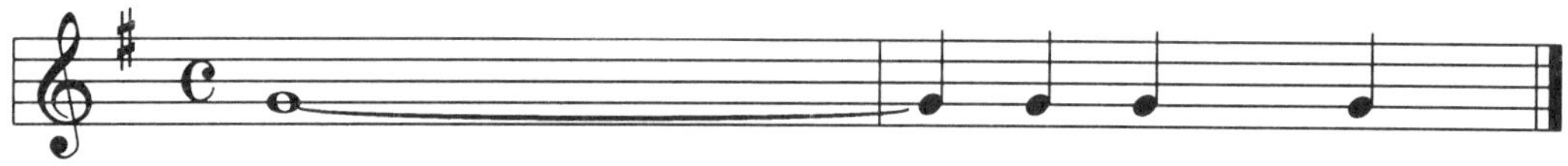

LEFT HAND CHORD CHART

Play one octave lower

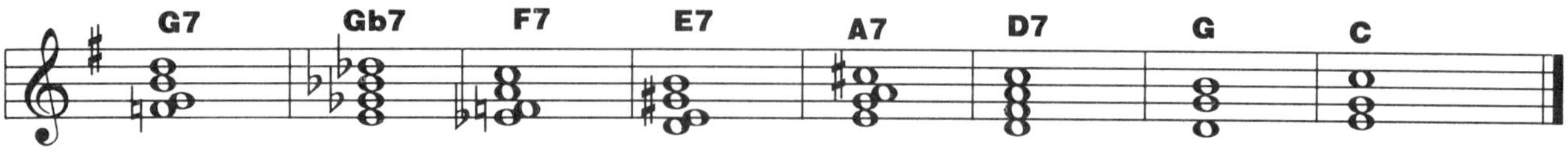

*Song & Chord Studies**

These studies will develop a sense of harmony.

** Note: REPEAT each STUDY until you know the NOTES in the CHORDS!*

I AIN'T GOT NOBODY

LEFT HAND CHORD CHART

Play one octave lower

NANCY MUSIC CO. INC. COPYRIGHT 1998

I LOVE YOU TRULY

Basic Rhythm

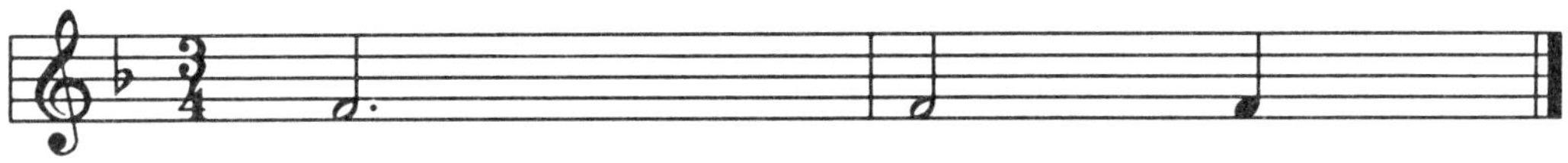

LEFT HAND CHORD CHART

Play one octave lower

*"I LOVE YOU TRULY" Song & Chord Studies **

These studies will develop a sense of harmony.

***** Note: REPEAT each STUDY until you know the NOTES in the CHORDS!***

I LOVE YOU TRULY

LEFT HAND CHORD CHART

Play one octave lower

NANCY MUSIC CO. INC. COPYRIGHT 1998

I NEVER KNEW

Basic Rhythm

LEFT HAND CHORD CHART

Play one octave lower

*"I NEVER KNEW" Song & Chord Studies**

<u>These studies will develop a sense of harmony.</u>

*** Note: REPEAT each STUDY until you know the NOTES in the CHORDS!***

I NEVER KNEW

LEFT HAND CHORD CHART

Play one octave lower

NANCY MUSIC CO. INC. COPYRIGHT 1998

I WANT A GIRL

Basic Rhythm

LEFT HAND CHORD CHART

Play one octave lower

Song & Chord Studies

These studies will develop a sense of harmony.

*** Note: REPEAT each STUDY until you know the NOTES in the CHORDS!**

I WANT A GIRL

LEFT HAND CHORD CHART

Play one octave lower

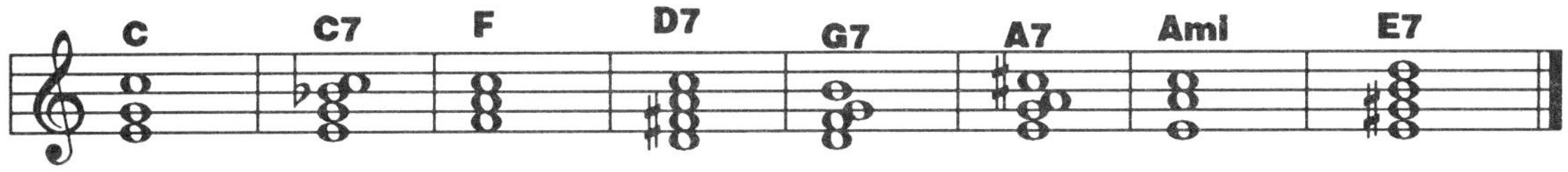

NANCY MUSIC CO. INC. COPYRIGHT C 1998

I'M FALLING IN LOVE WITH SOMEONE

Basic Rhythm

LEFT HAND CHORD CHART

Play one octave lower

*"I'M FALLING IN LOVE" Song & Chord Studies**

<u>These studies will develop a sense of harmony.</u>

***Note: REPEAT each STUDY until you know the NOTES in the CHORDS!**

I'M FALLING IN LOVE WITH SOMEONE

LEFT HAND CHORD CHART

Play one octave lower

NANCY MUSIC CO. INC. COPYRIGHT 1998

I'M FOREVER BLOWING BUBBLES

Basic Rhythm

LEFT HAND CHORD CHART

Play one octave lower

"I'M FOREVER BLOWING" Song & Chord Studies

These studies will develop a sense of harmony.

SONG---- *CHORDS----*

*** Note: REPEAT each STUDY until you know the NOTES in the CHORDS!**

I'M FOREVER BLOWING BUBBLES

LEFT HAND CHORD CHART

Play one octave lower

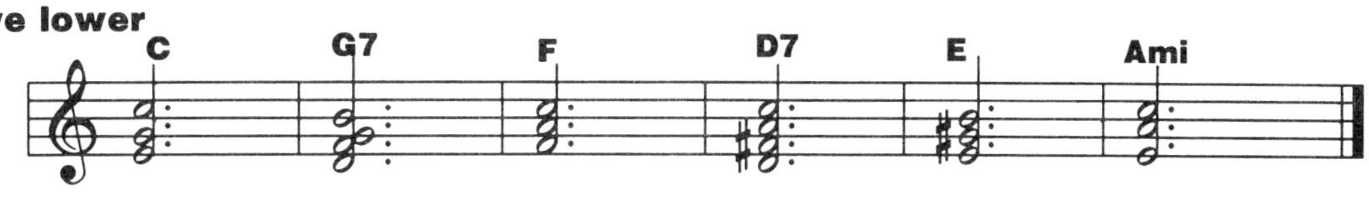

NANCY MUSIC CO. INC. COPYRIGHT 1998

IF I HAD MY WAY

Basic Rhythm

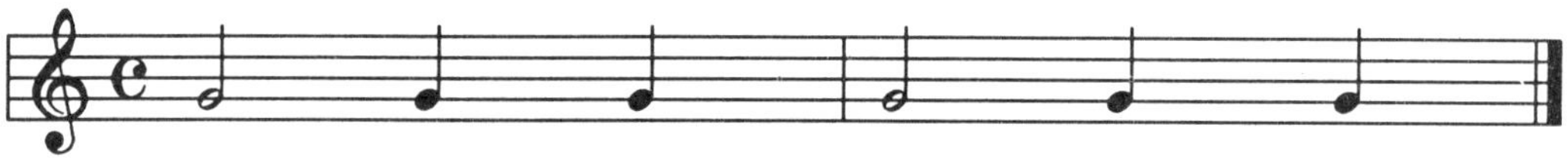

LEFT HAND CHORD CHART

Play one octave lower

*"IF I HAD MY WAY" Song & Chord Studies **

These studies will develop a sense of harmony.

** Note: REPEAT each STUDY until you know the NOTES in the CHORDS!*

IF HAD MY WAY

LEFT HAND CHORD CHART

Play one octave lower

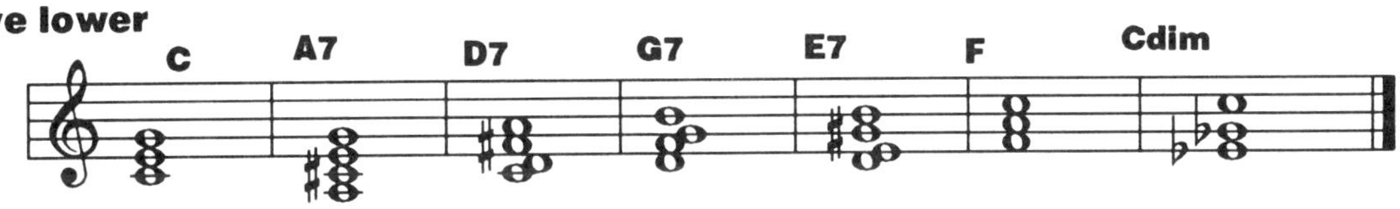

NANCY MUSIC CO. INC. COPYRIGHT 1998

(BACK HOME AGAIN IN) INDIANA

Basic Rhythm

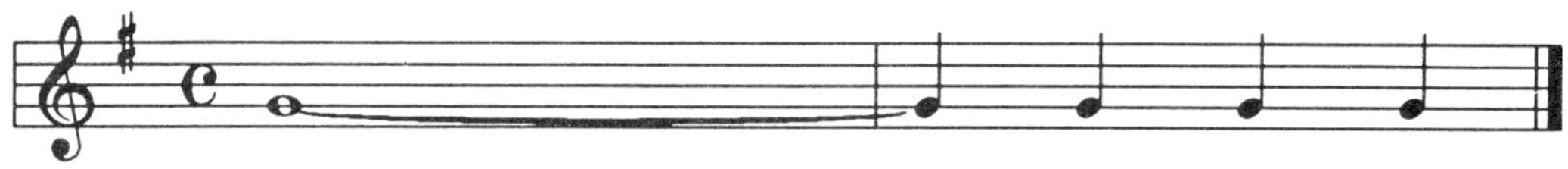

LEFT HAND CHORD CHART

Play one octave lower

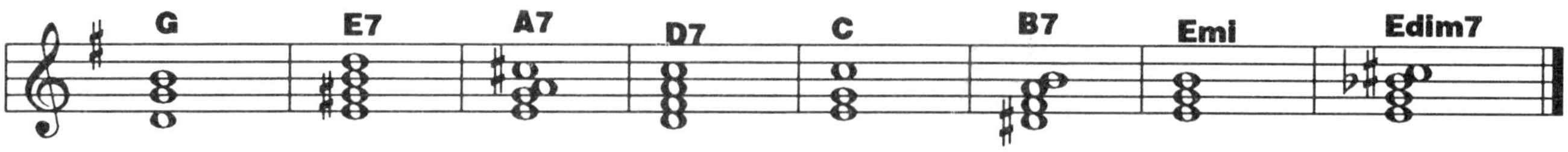

Song & Chord Studies

These studies will develop a sense of harmony.

**** Note: REPEAT each STUDY until you know the NOTES in the CHORDS!***

(BACK HOME AGAIN IN) INDIANA

LEFT HAND CHORD CHART

Play one octave lower

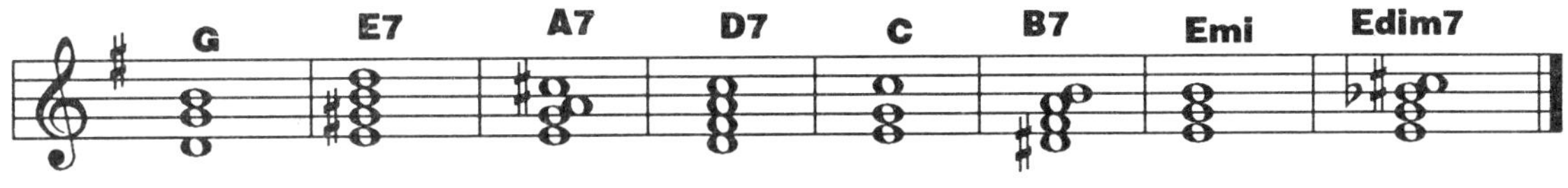

NANCY MUSIC CO. INC. COPYRIGHT C 1998

JA-DA

Basic Rhythm

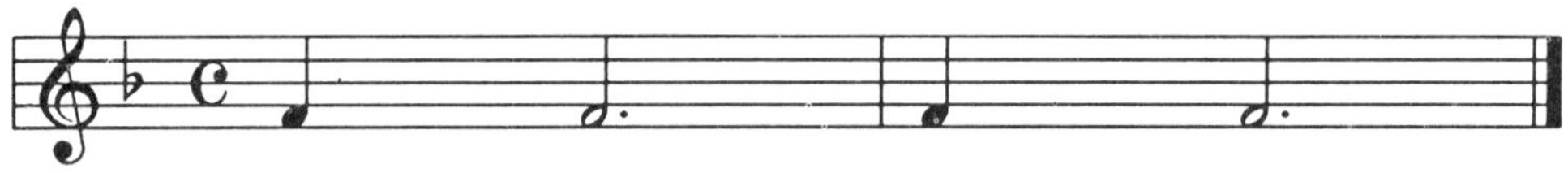

LEFT HAND CHORD CHART

Play one octave lower

*"JA-DA" Song & Chord Studies**

These studies will develop a sense of harmony.

SONG---- ***CHORDS----***

**** Note: REPEAT each STUDY until you know the NOTES in the CHORDS!***

JA-DA

LEFT HAND CHORD CHART

Play one octave lower

NANCY MUSIC CO. INC. COPYRIGHT 1998

LET ME CALL YOU SWEETHEART

Basic Rhythm

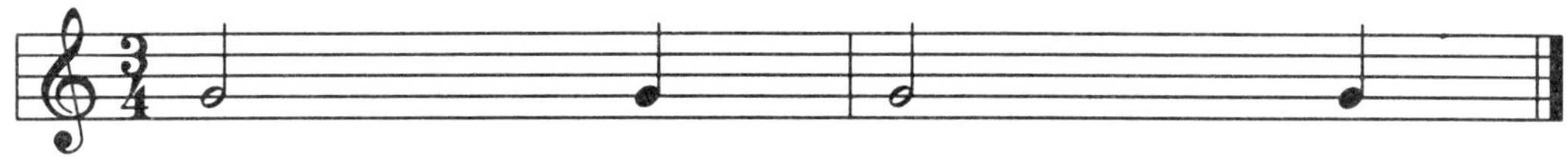

LEFT HAND CHORD CHART

Play one octave lower

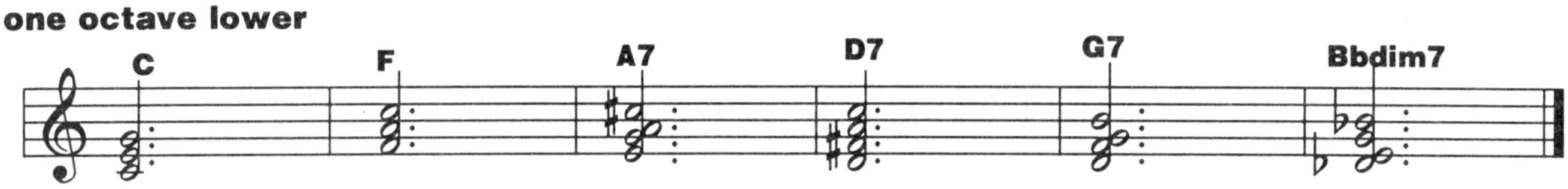

"LET ME CALL YOU " Song & Chord Studies

<u>These studies will develop a sense of harmony.</u>

**** Note: REPEAT each STUDY until you know the NOTES in the CHORDS!***

LET ME CALL YOU SWEETHEART

LEFT HAND CHORD CHART

Play one octave lower

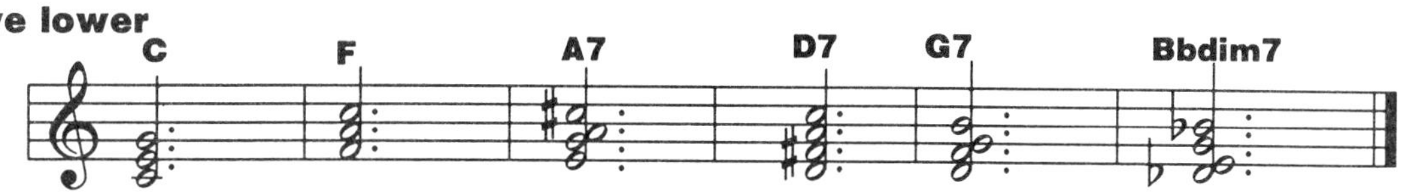

NANCY MUSIC CO. INC. COPYRIGHT 1998

MARGIE

Basic Rhythm

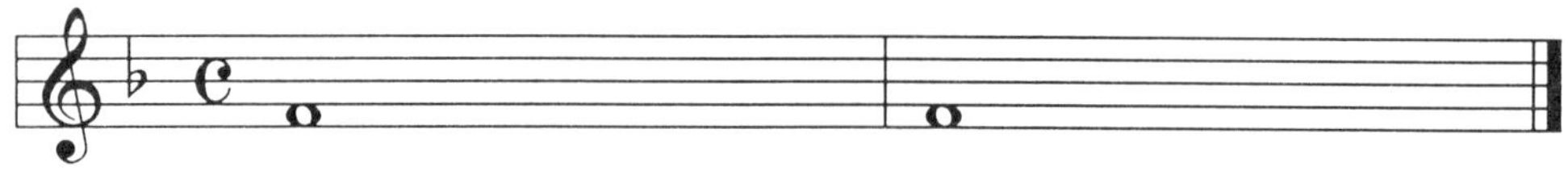

LEFT HAND CHORD CHART

Play one octave lower

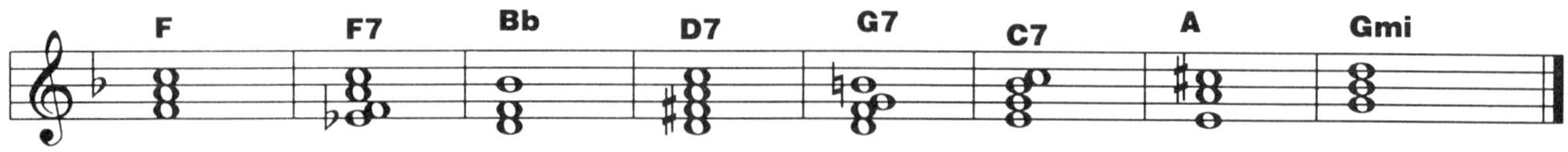

*"MARGIE" Song & Chord Studies**

These studies will develop a sense of harmony.

*** Note: REPEAT each STUDY until you know the NOTES in the CHORDS!***

MARGIE

LEFT HAND CHORD CHART

Play one octave lower

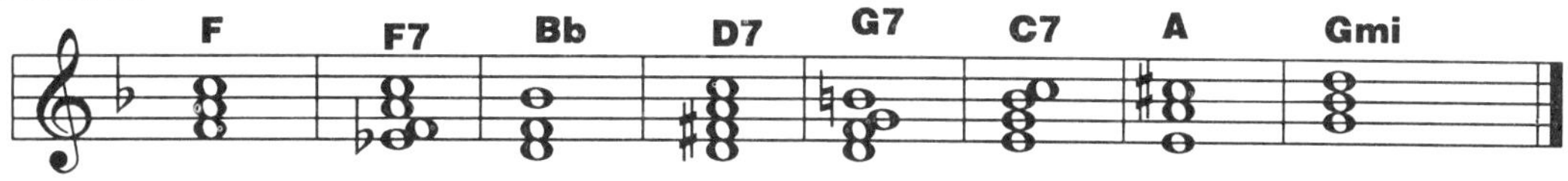

NANCY MUSIC CO. INC. COPYRIGHT 1998

MEMORIES

Basic Rhythm

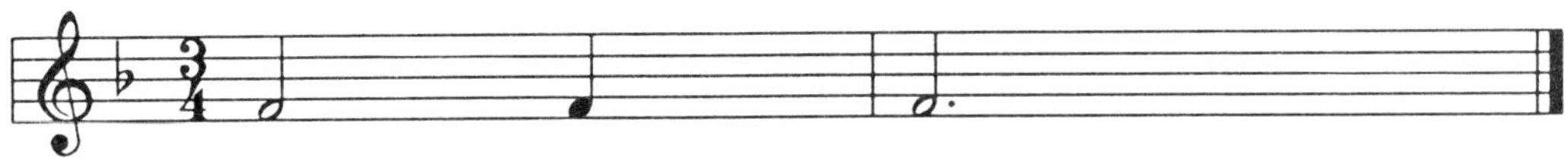

LEFT HAND CHORD CHART

Play one octave lower

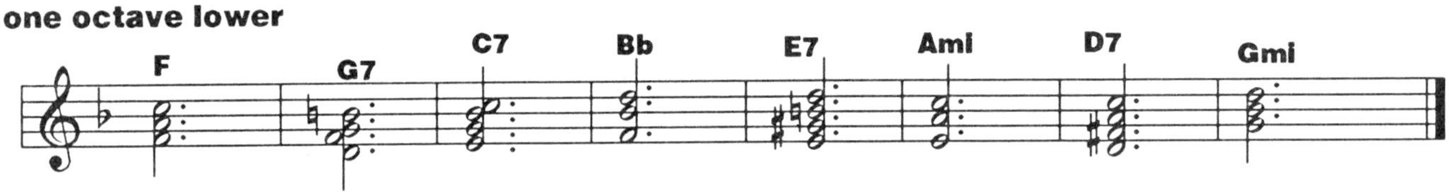

"MEMORIES" Song & Chord Studies *

These studies will develop a sense of harmony.

*** Note: REPEAT each STUDY until you know the NOTES in the CHORDS!**

MEMORIES

LEFT HAND CHORD CHART

Play one octave lower

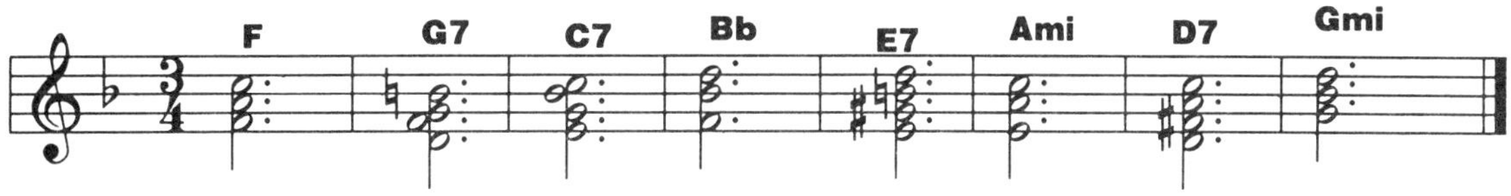

NANCY MUSIC CO. INC. COPYRIGHT C 1998

MELANCHOLY BABY

Basic Rhythm

LEFT HAND CHORD CHART

Play one octave lower

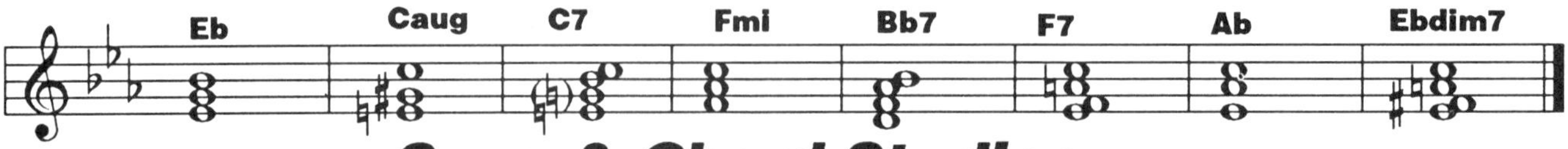

Song & Chord Studies

These studies will develop a sense of harmony.

**** Note: REPEAT each STUDY until you know the NOTES in the CHORDS!***

MELANCHOLY BABY

LEFT HAND CHORD CHART

Play one octave lower

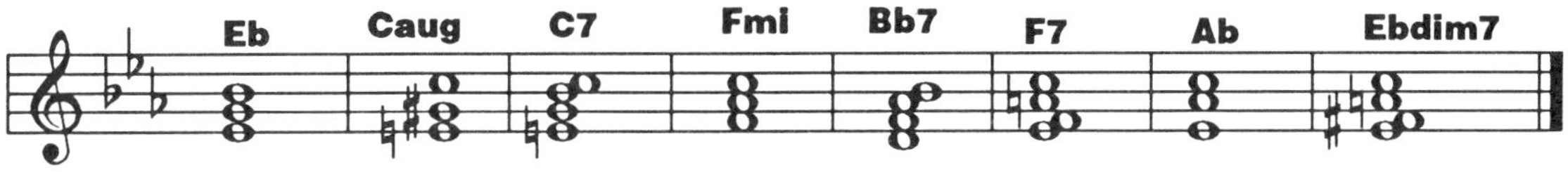

NANCY MUSIC CO. INC. COPYRIGHT C 1998

OH, YOU BEAUTIFUL DOLL

Basic Rhythm

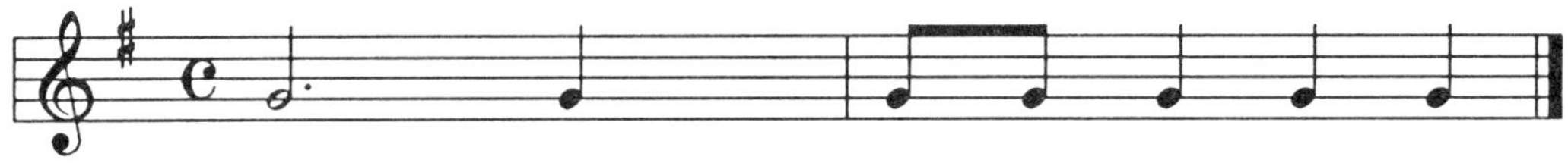

LEFT HAND CHORD CHART

Play one octave lower

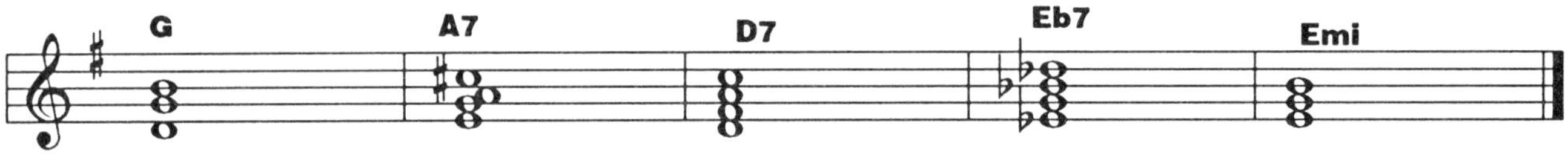

*"OH, YOU BEAUTIFUL DOLL" Song & Chord Studies **

<u>These studies will develop a sense of harmony.</u>

SONG---- ***CHORDS----***

** Note: REPEAT each STUDY until you know the NOTES in the CHORDS!*

OH, YOU BEAUTIFUL DOLL

LEFT HAND CHORD CHART

Play one octave lower

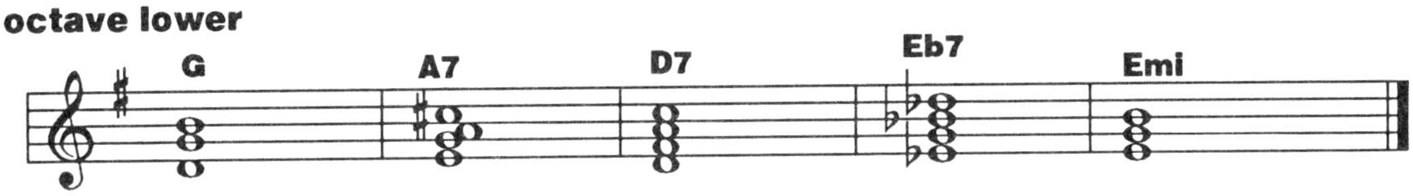

NANCY MUSIC CO. INC. COPYRIGHT C 1998

ON A SUNDAY AFTERNOON

Basic Rhythm

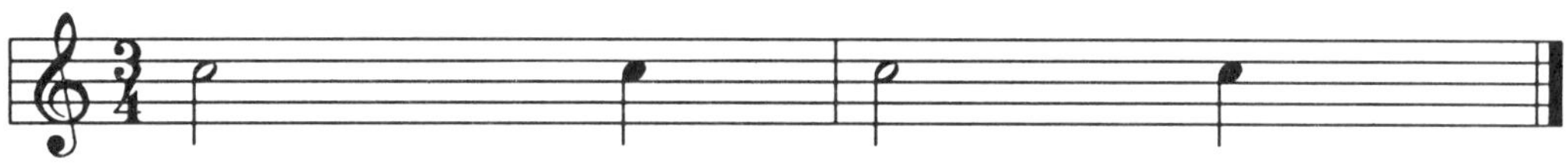

LEFT HAND CHORD CHART

Play one octave lower

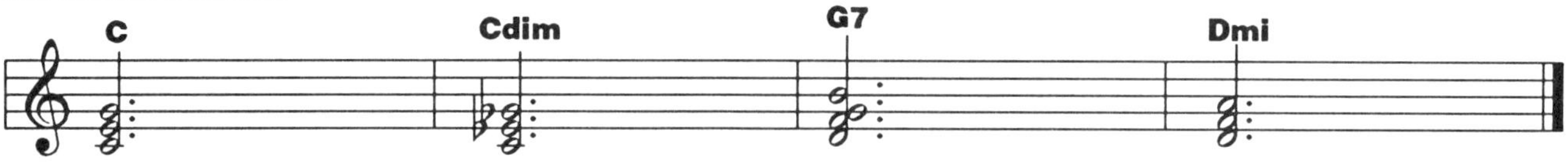

*"ON A SUNDAY AFTERNOON" Song & Chord Studies **

These studies will develop a sense of harmony.

*** Note: REPEAT each STUDY until you know the NOTES in the CHORDS!***

ON A SUNDAY AFTERNOON

LEFT HAND CHORD CHART

Play one octave lower

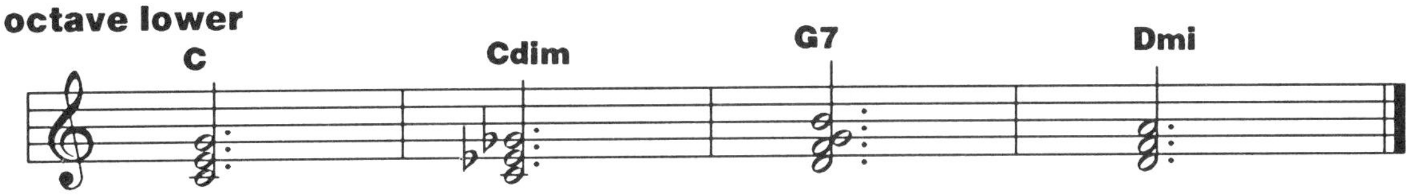

NANCY MUSIC CO. INC. COPYRIGHT C 1998

PEG OF MY HEART

Basic Rhythm

LEFT HAND CHORD CHART

Play one octave lower

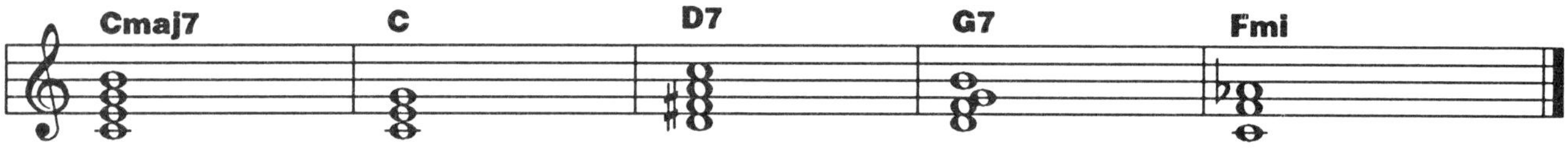

*"PEG OF MY HEART" Song & Chord Studies **

<u>These studies will develop a sense of harmony.</u>

**** Note: REPEAT each STUDY until you know the NOTES in the CHORDS!***

PEG OF MY HEART

LEFT HAND CHORD CHART

Play one octave lower

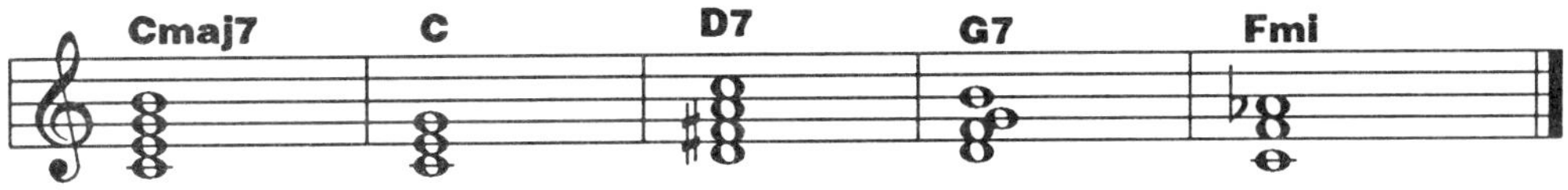

NANCY MUSIC CO. INC. COPYRIGHT 1998

POOR BUTTERFLY

Basic Rhythm

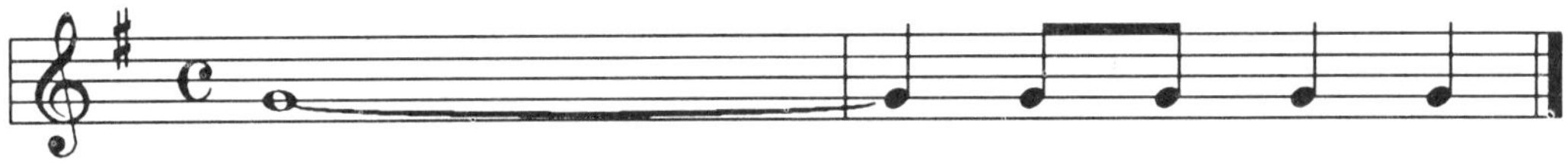

LEFT HAND CHORD CHART

Play one octave lower

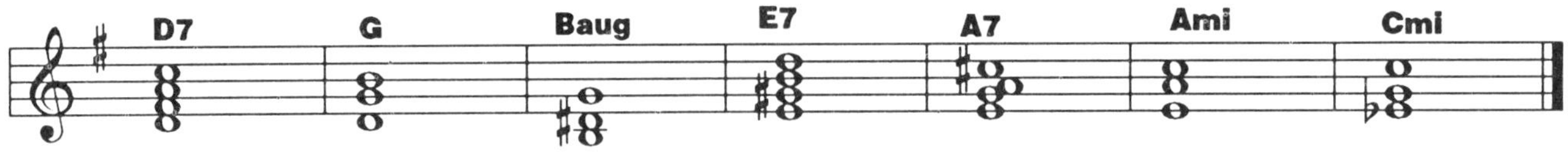

*"POOR BUTTERFLY" Song & Chord Studies **

These studies will develop a sense of harmony.

*** Note: REPEAT each STUDY until you know the NOTES in the CHORDS!***

POOR BUTTERFLY

LEFT HAND CHORD CHART

Play one octave lower

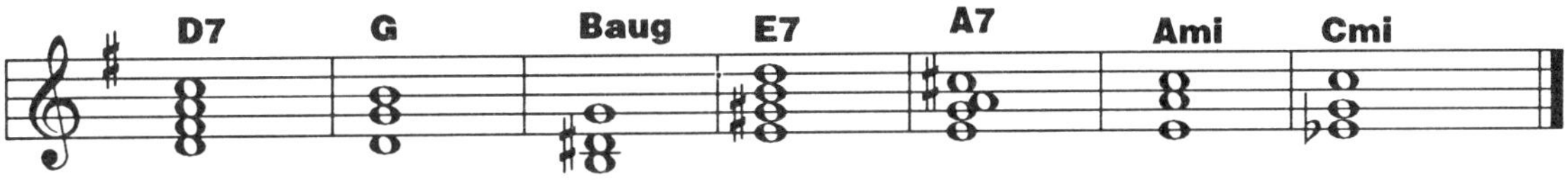

NANCY MUSIC CO. INC. COPYRIGHT C 1998

PRETTY BABY

Basic Rhythm

LEFT HAND CHORD CHART

Play one octave lower

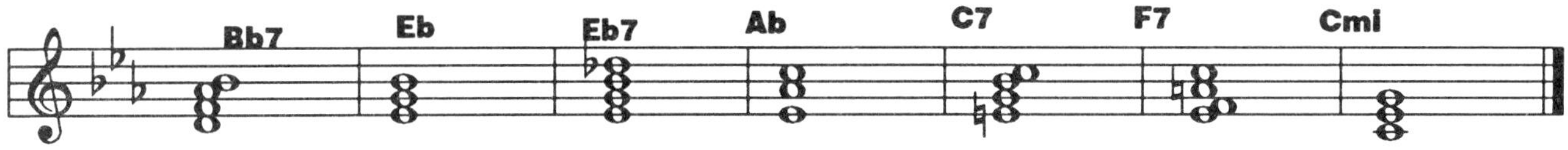

*"PRETTY BABY" Song & Chord Studies **

These studies will develop a sense of harmony.

**** Note: REPEAT each STUDY until you know the NOTES in the CHORDS!***

PRETTY BABY

LEFT HAND CHORD CHART

Play one octave lower

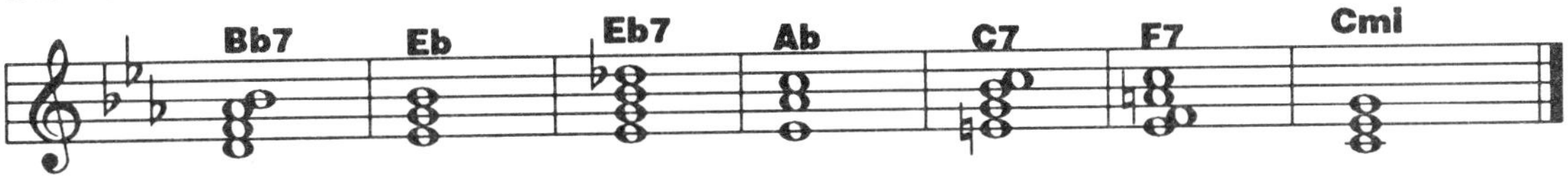

NANCY MUSIC CO. INC. COPYRIGHT C 1998

PUT YOUR ARMS AROUND ME, HONEY

Basic Rhythm

LEFT HAND CHORD CHART

Play one octave lower

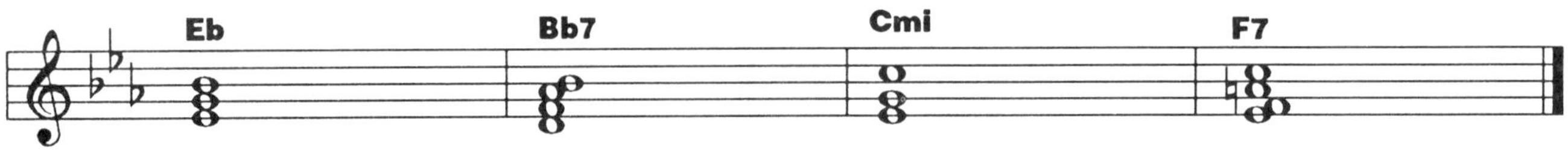

'PUT YOUR ARMS AROUND ME" Song & Chord Studies

These studies will develop a sense of harmony.

**** Note: REPEAT each STUDY until you know the NOTES in the CHORDS!***

PUT YOUR ARMS AROUND ME, HONEY

LEFT HAND CHORD CHART

Play one octave lower

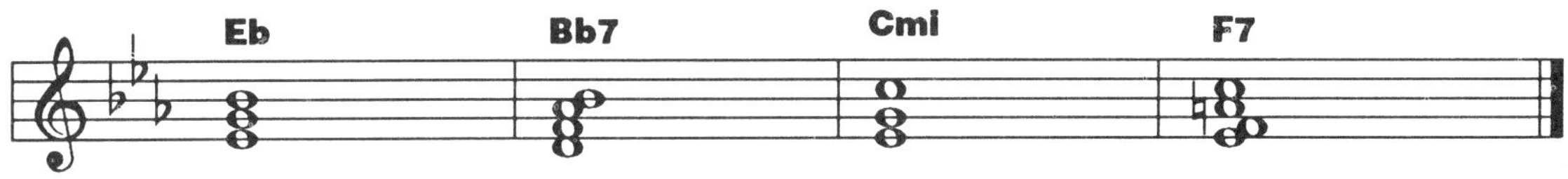

NANCY MUSIC CO. INC. COPYRIGHT C 1998

ROYAL GARDEN BLUES

Basic Rhythm

LEFT HAND CHORD CHART

Play one octave lower

*"ROYAL GARDEN BLUES" Song & Chord Studies **

<u>These studies will develop a sense of harmony.</u>

SONG---- ***CHORDS----***

** Note: REPEAT each STUDY until you know the NOTES in the CHORDS!*

ROYAL GARDEN BLUES

LEFT HAND CHORD CHART

Play one octave lower

NANCY MUSIC CO. INC. COPYRIGHT 1998

SOMEBODY STOLE MY GAL

LEFT HAND CHORD CHART

Play one octave lower

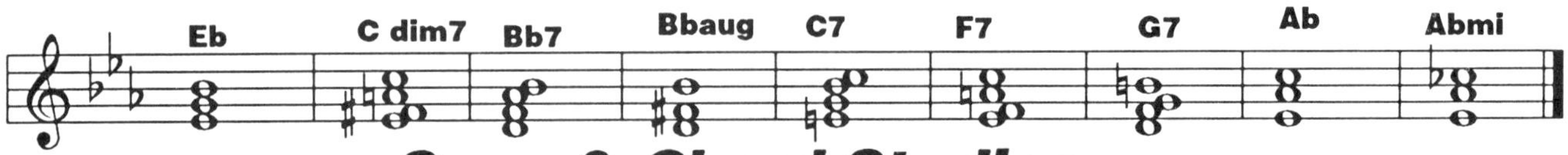

Song & Chord Studies

These studies will develop a sense of harmony.

**** Note: REPEAT each STUDY until you know the NOTES in the CHORDS!***

SOMEBODY STOLE MY GAL

LEFT HAND CHORD CHART

Play one octave lower

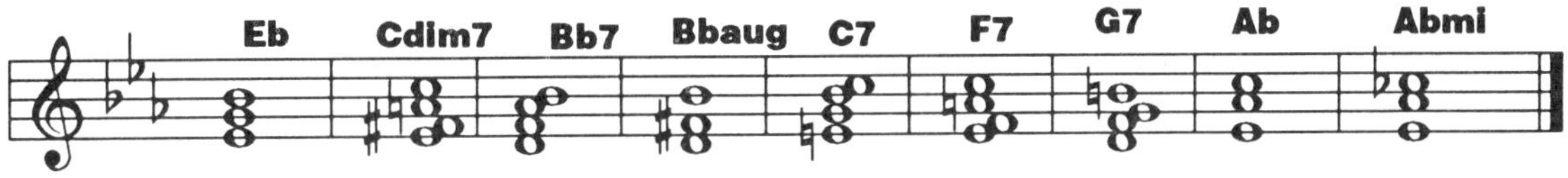

NANCY MUSIC CO. INC. COPYRIGHT C 1998

ST. LOUIS BLUES

Basic Rhythm

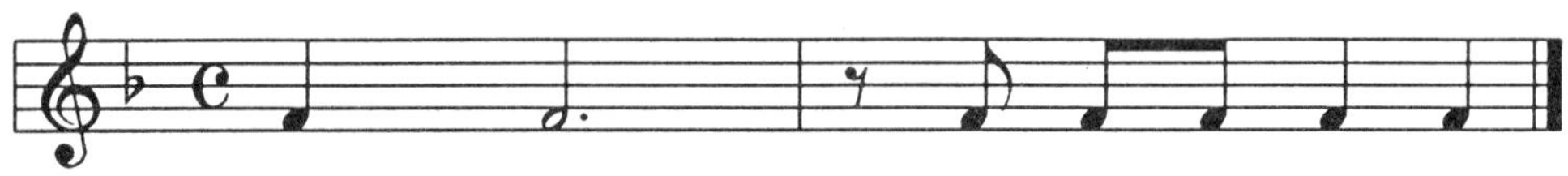

LEFT HAND CHORD CHART

Play one octave lower

*"ST. LOUIS BLUES" Song & Chord Studies**

These studies will develop a sense of harmony.

SONG---- ***CHORDS----***

**** Note: REPEAT each STUDY until you know the NOTES in the CHORDS!***

ST. LOUIS BLUES

LEFT HAND CHORD CHART

Play one octave lower

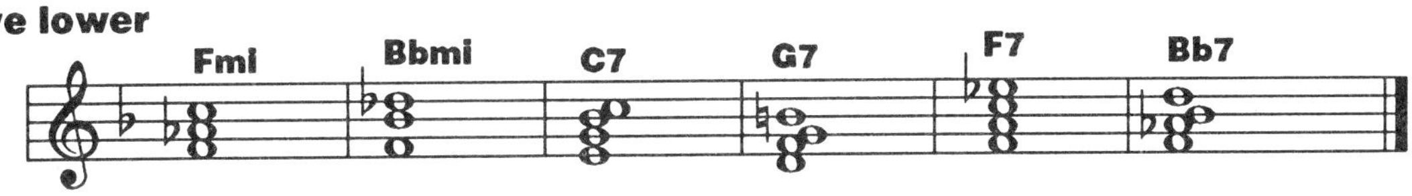

NANCY MUSIC CO. INC. COPYRIGHT 1998

SWANEE

Basic Rhythm

LEFT HAND CHORD CHART

Play one octave lower

*"SWANEE" Song & Chord Studies**

These studies will develop a sense of harmony.

****Note: REPEAT each STUDY until you know the NOTES in the CHORDS!***

SWANEE

LEFT HAND CHORD CHART

Play one octave lower

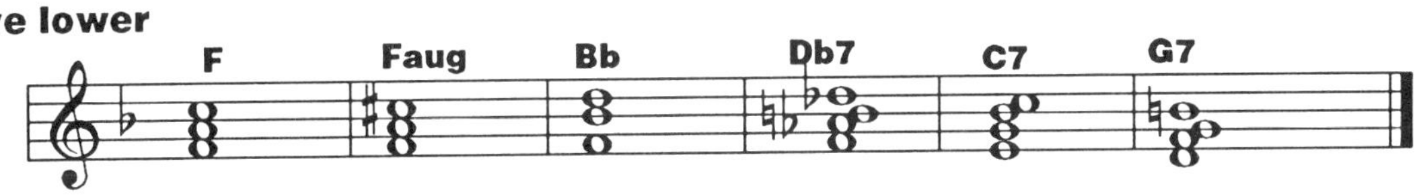

NANCY MUSIC CO. INC. COPYRIGHT 1998

THE BELLS OF ST. MARY'S

Basic Rhythm

LEFT HAND CHORD CHART

Play one octave lower

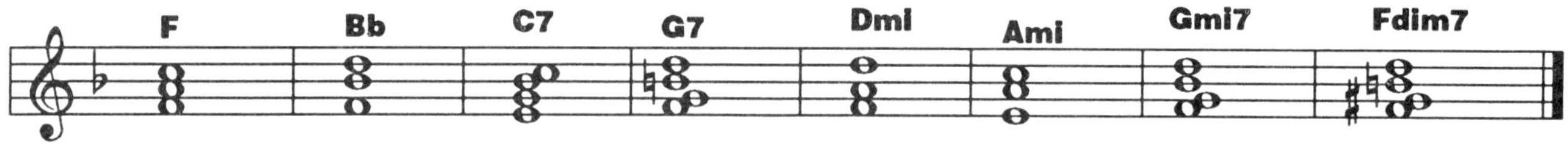

*"THE BELLS OF ST. MARY'S" Song & Chord Studies**

<u>These studies will develop a sense of harmony.</u>

**** Note: REPEAT each STUDY until you know the NOTES in the CHORDS!***

THE BELLS OF ST. MARY'S

LEFT HAND CHORD CHART

Play one octave lower

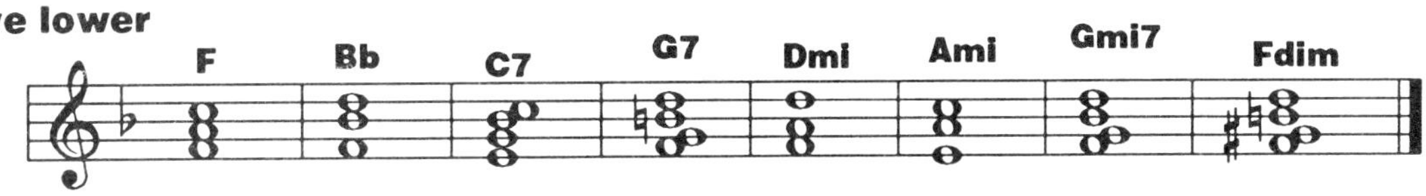

NANCY MUSIC CO. INC. COPYRIGHT 1998

THE SHEIK OF ARABY

Basic Rhythm

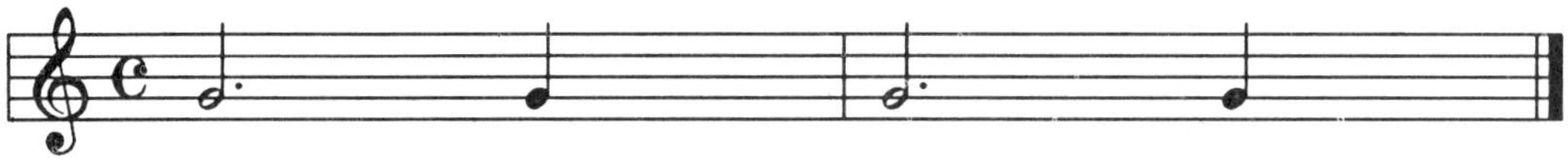

LEFT HAND CHORD CHART

Play one octave lower

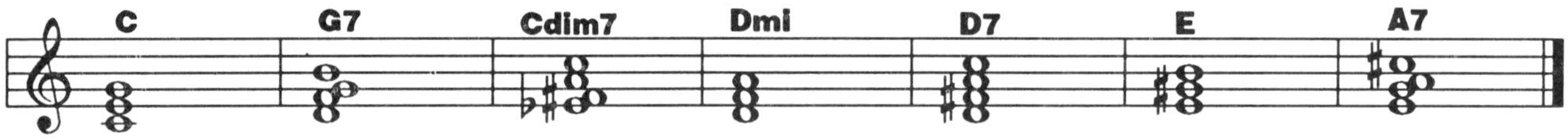

*"THE SHEIK OF ARABY" Song & Chord Studies **

These studies will develop a sense of harmony.

SONG---- ***CHORDS----***

**** Note: REPEAT each STUDY until you know the NOTES in the CHORDS!***

THE SHEIK OF ARABY

LEFT HAND CHORD CHART

Play one octave lower

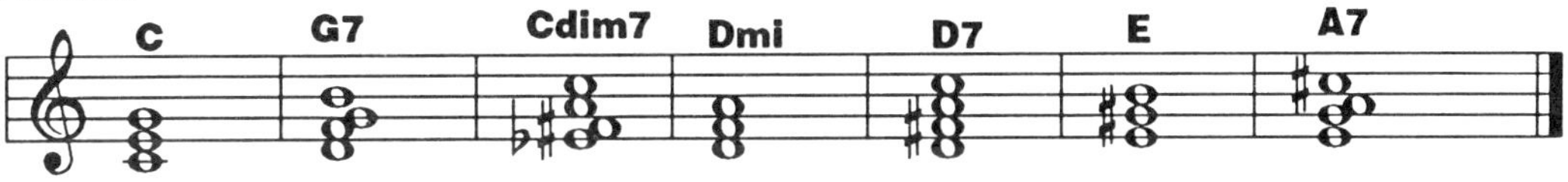

NANCY MUSIC CO. INC. COPYRIGHT 1998

THE YELLOW ROSE OF TEXAS

Basic Rhythm

LEFT HAND CHORD CHART

Play one octave lower

Song & Chord Studies

These studies will develop a sense of harmony.

SONG---- **CHORDS----**

**** Note: REPEAT each STUDY until you know the NOTES in the CHORDS!***

THE YELLOW ROSE OF TEXAS

LEFT HAND CHORD CHART

Play one octave lower

NANCY MUSIC CO. INC. COPYRIGHT C 1998

TIGER RAG

Basic Rhythm

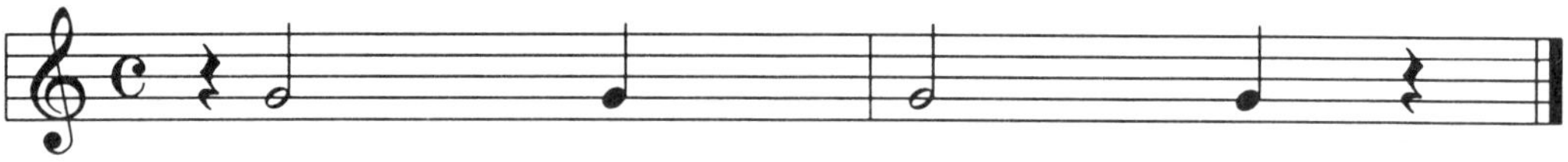

LEFT HAND CHORD CHART

Play one octave lower

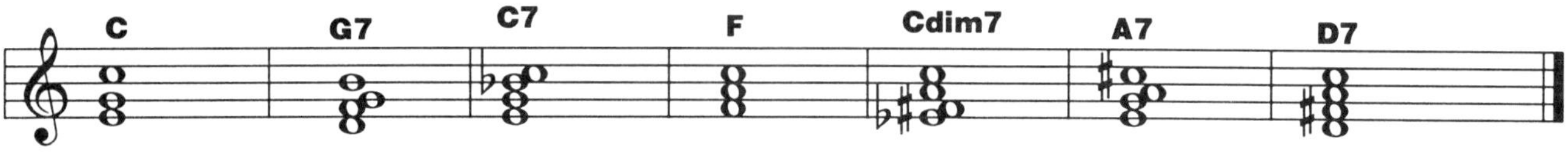

Song & Chord Studies

These studies will develop a sense of harmony.

**** Note: REPEAT each STUDY until you know the NOTES in the CHORDS!***

TIGER RAG

LEFT HAND CHORD CHART

Play one octave lower

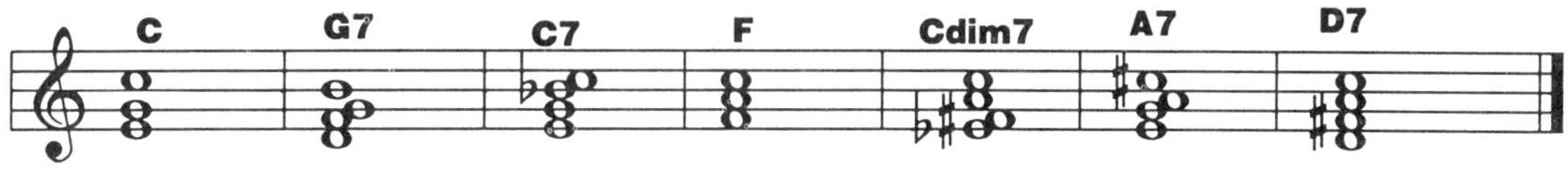

NANCY MUSIC CO. INC. COPYRIGHT C 1998

WHEN IRISH EYES ARE SMILING

Basic Rhythm

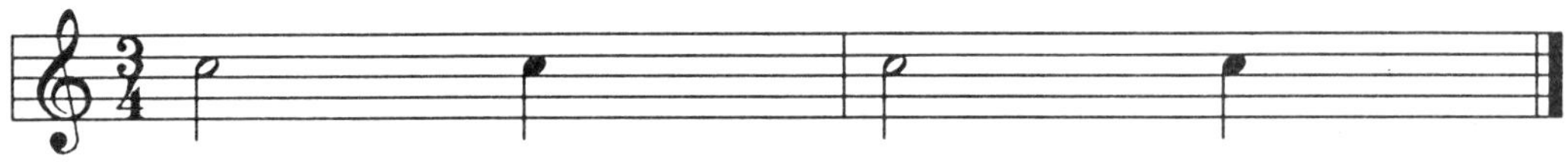

LEFT HAND CHORD CHART

Play one octave lower

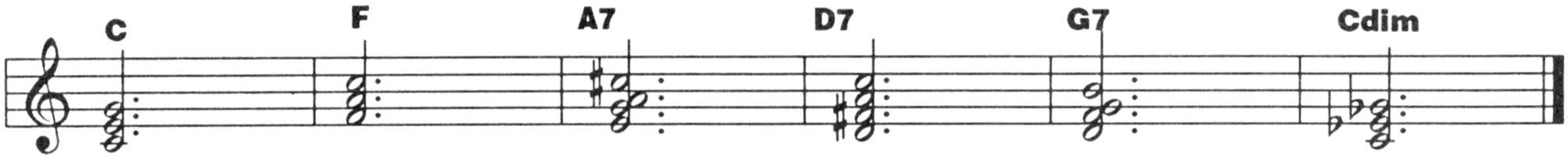

*"WHEN IRISH EYES" Song & Chord Studies **

<u>These studies will develop a sense of harmony.</u>

**** Note: REPEAT each STUDY until you know the NOTES in the CHORDS!***

WHEN IRISH EYES ARE SMILING

LEFT HAND CHORD CHART

Play one octave lower

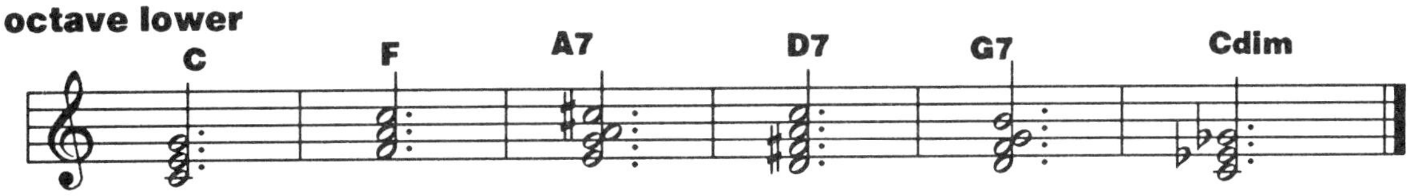

NANCY MUSIC CO. INC. COPYRIGHT C 1998

WHEN YOU WERE SWEET SIXTEEN

Basic Rhythm

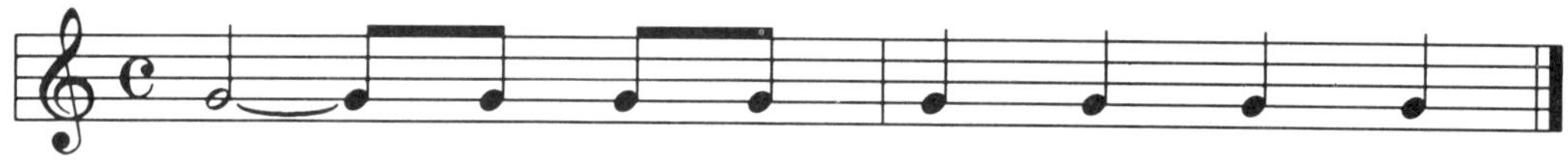

LEFT HAND CHORD CHART

Play one octave lower

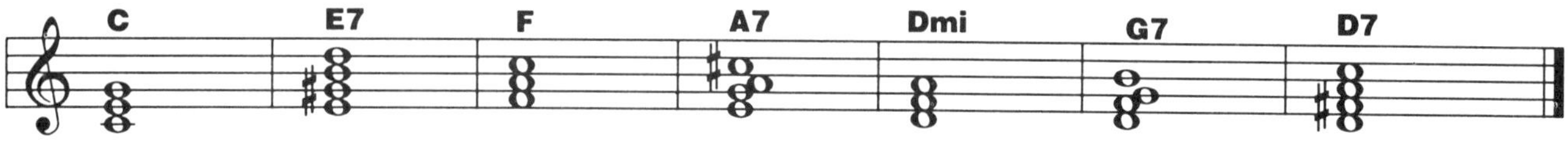

Song & Chord Studies

These studies will develop a sense of harmony.

** Note: REPEAT each STUDY until you know the NOTES in the CHORDS!*

WHEN YOU WERE SWEET SIXTEEN

LEFT HAND CHORD CHART

Play one octave lower

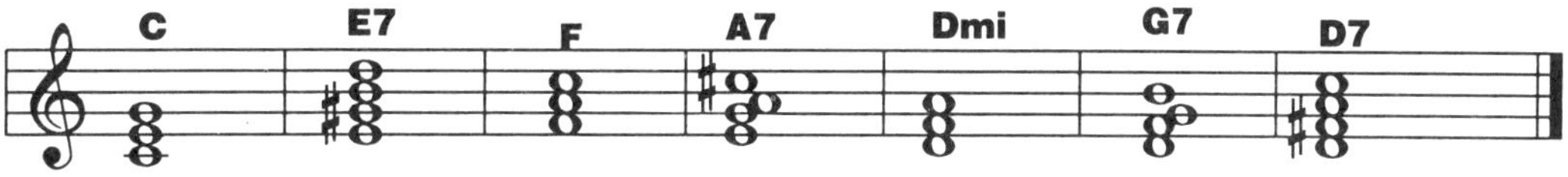

NANCY MUSIC CO. INC. COPYRIGHT 1998

WHISPERING

Basic Rhythm

LEFT HAND CHORD CHART

Play one octave lower

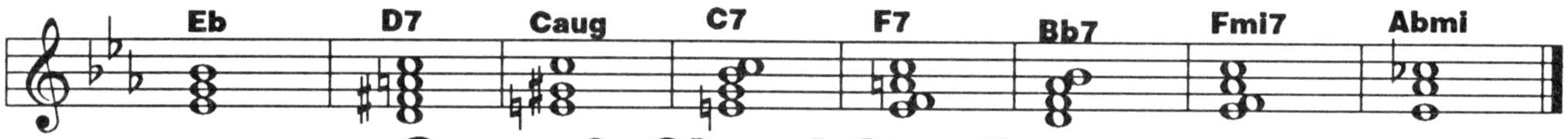

Song & Chord Studies

These studies will develop a sense of harmony.

SONG---- **CHORDS----**

**** Note: REPEAT each STUDY until you know the NOTES in the CHORDS!***

WHISPERING

LEFT HAND CHORD CHART

Play one octave lower

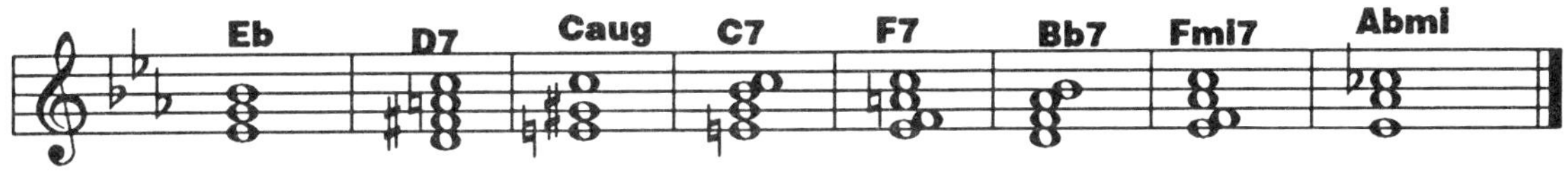

NANCY MUSIC CO. INC. COPYRIGHT C 1998

YOU MADE ME LOVE YOU

Basic Rhythm

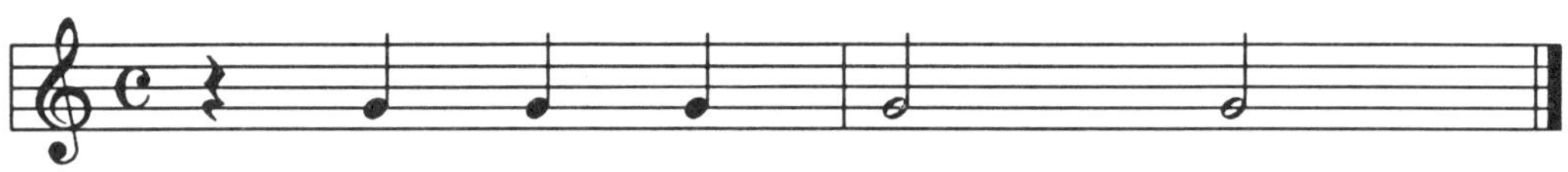

LEFT HAND CHORD CHART

Play one octave lower

Song & Chord Studies

These studies will develop a sense of harmony.

**** Note: REPEAT each STUDY until you know the NOTES in the CHORDS!***

YOU MADE ME LOVE YOU

LEFT HAND CHORD CHART

Play one octave lower

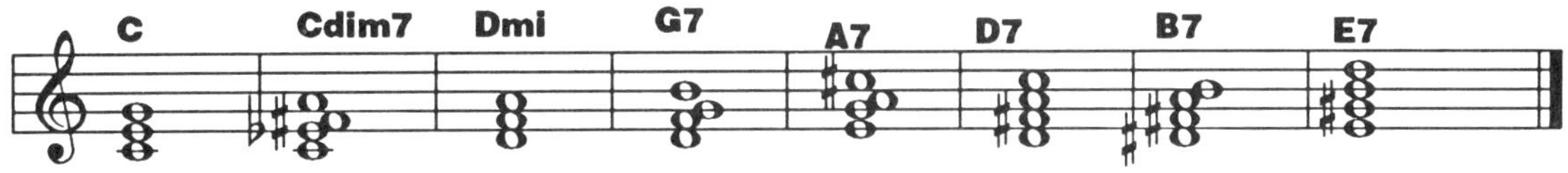

NANCY MUSIC CO. INC. COPYRIGHT C 1998